simple faith

Other Books by Margaret Silf

Close to the Heart: A Guide to Personal Prayer

Going on Retreat: A Beginner's Guide to the Christian Retreat Experience

Inner Compass: An Invitation to Ignatian Spirituality

Compass Points: Meeting God Every Day at Every Turn

The Other Side of Chaos

simple faith

moving beyond religion as you know it
to grow in your relationship with God

Margaret Silf

LOYOLA PRESS.
A JESUIT MINISTRY
Chicago

LOYOLA PRESS.
A JESUIT MINISTRY

3441 N. Ashland Avenue
Chicago, Illinois 60657
(800) 621-1008
www.loyolapress.com

Scripture quotations contained herein are from the New Revised Standard Version Bible: Catholic Edition, copyright © 1993 and 1989 by the Division of Christian Education of the National Council of the Churches of Christ in the U.S.A. Used by permission. All rights reserved.

First published in 2011 as *Faith* by Darton, Longman and Todd Ltd, 1 Spencer Court, 140–142 Wandsworth High Street, London SW18 4JJ, © 2011 Margaret Silf. The right of Margaret Silf to be identified as the author of this work has been asserted in accordance with the Copyright, Designs and Patents Act 1998. ISBN: 978-0-232-52794-0 A catalogue record for this book is available from the British Library.

Art credit: © Frank Lukasseck/Photographer's Choice/Getty Images

Library of Congress Cataloging-in-Publication Data

Silf, Margaret.
  Simple faith / Margaret Silf.
    p. cm.
  ISBN-13: 978-0-8294-3623-5
  ISBN-10: 0-8294-3623-5
1. Faith--Meditations. I. Title.
  BV4637.S52 2012
  234'.23—dc23

                                                              2011038162

Printed in the United States of America
      13 14 15 16 Bang 10 9 8 7 6 5 4 3

Contents

Introduction

My baby granddaughter has more faith than I do:

- She believes that when I am holding her I won't drop her.

- She believes that when she is hungry someone will feed her.

- She believes that life and the world mean well for her.

- She believes—indeed I hope she *knows*—that we love her.

- She doesn't think about "faith"—she just lives it.

- As she grows older, her faith will become more complicated.

She will learn that sometimes life will let her down and she will get hurt.

She will discover that not every need is going to be met just because she shouts loudly enough.

She will learn to distinguish between those things in life—kindness, compassion, justice, and truth—that are making her, and all of us, more fully alive and those things such as war and greed and selfishness that are working against the fullness of life.

She will come to understand that faith is a cooperative venture and that her own actions and choices have reactions and results.

She will try to work things out, try to pin things down and get a grasp on her life's meaning.

She will hear many conflicting voices and may come to think that faith is hard work, an intellectual marathon, or a puzzle to be gnawed at until a solution emerges.

Then one day—please, God—she will become older and wiser. By then she will have learned that the hurts along the way will have made her stronger, clarified her inner truth, and revealed her own limitations.

She will concede that sometimes, after all, God knew best and that good things grow from seeds that have been broken open by the weather and have lain hidden in the dark earth. She will look back over the kaleidoscope of her life and notice how the fragments of experience that made no sense at the time were, all along, shaping a rather beautiful pattern.

The faith she has then will be simple again. But it will have a simplicity born of experience and reflection, a simplicity that looks back with gratitude on all she has seen and done and lived, a simplicity that is confident in trusting God for all that remains unseen, undone, and unlived. It will be the kind of faith that knows that God is more likely to ask her, at the end of her journey, "How well did you love?" than "How much did you understand?" And her answer might be:

- Someone trusted me, and I didn't let him down.

- Someone was hungry, and I fed her.

- Someone was hopeless, and I gave him a reason to trust that at least one person meant well for him.

- Someone had no one, and I loved her.

It sounds simple. But it takes a lifetime to reach that simplicity and to come full circle, from infant faith to mature faith, from the source of our being to its destiny.

Having simple faith is simply to journey in trust, like a baby, but with the wounds and scars of an adult, like a man who died on a cross and who invited us to "become like children" (Matthew 18:3). When we follow him, we discover that his footsteps lead right back, full circle, to a whole new beginning.

1
Who Is God for Me?

A little girl in kindergarten was painting a picture. Her teacher asked, "What are you painting?"

The child replied, "It's a picture of God."

Very interested to see what the result would be, the teacher commented, "But nobody knows what God looks like."

"They will when I have finished my picture."

We all have our "pictures of God," and most of them started to form in early childhood. Of course no one has seen God. So it follows that any picture, or image, of God that we form is going to be completely inadequate or even seriously harmful.

These *unhelpful* images are familiar to many of us:

- God the strict parent or schoolteacher, waiting to catch us in wrongdoing and punish us

- God the firefighter, who comes to the rescue when we are in trouble

- God the Santa Claus, who delivers the items on our wish list

- God the warrior or commander, who fights on our side in every battle and vanquishes our enemies

- God the demanding employer, who expects us to work all hours and rarely gives us a bonus

All these pictures have one thing in common: they image God as a person, like us, only bigger and more powerful. Because we are human, it's inevitable that, like the little girl, we make pictures of God that look like ourselves, since this is all we know. But could we do better than this? Can our image of God grow up a bit now that we are grown up ourselves?

Some Alternative Images

Mystics through the ages have struggled to express their sense of God in more abstract ways:

- The Word who calls creation into being

- The Energy of all life

- The deep Wisdom underlying all that exists

- The Spirit who holds us in being and guides us

- The Light in which all is known and understood and that outshines all our shadows

Quakers speak of "that which is of God within all beings." And St. Ignatius speaks of "finding God in all things."

Jesuit priest Anthony de Mello tells the story of the fish that was searching for the mystery he called Ocean. "Where is Ocean?" he asked every other fish he met. Nobody could tell him. "What does Ocean look like?" Nobody could say; nobody had ever seen it.

Perhaps the fish went on his way, dismissing the idea of Ocean as a figment of the collective imagination.

Or perhaps he realized that Ocean was the fullness of the mystery in which he and all the creatures of the deep live and move and have their being.

Many people would dismiss as a fiction the idea of God. Others intuit that God is the mystery in which we all live and move and have our being.

Do I Believe?

To be a person of faith is to believe that there is a power greater than ourselves, an all-powerful mystery in whom we live and move and have our being.

For the fish, the ocean is the medium that holds it afloat, that nourishes it and, by means of subtle movements and currents, guides its path. If the fish could leap out of the ocean, it would die. It isn't actually possible to leap out of the medium in which we have our being.

Nor is it possible to reject the reality of the mystery we call God. But it is possible, and sometimes necessary, to reject our own flawed and damaging images of God.

Try taking stock of some of your own images of God.

Are there any you feel you need to let go of?

Is there any image that really works for you?

Images can be helpful, but they are only images, only human attempts to describe what cannot be described. Let them help you in your faith journey, but don't let them imprison you.

A person of faith is someone who knows that he or she is not the center of the universe but acknowledges that faith, this center of gravity, lies in a mystery much deeper than human hearts can fathom—a mystery we call God.

What Do You Think?

When you say, "I believe in God," what do you mean?

> *God said to Moses, "I AM WHO I AM."*
> —Exodus 3:14

2
Relating to God

Human beings, like all mammals, are conceived, born, and live their lives in relationship. We are each a part of a vast and interdependent web of life in which every individual finds his or her meaning in the context of the whole.

We all know how challenging it can be to live in healthy and loving relationships. Relating to one another is the most demanding aspect of what it means to be human, but it is at the very heart of what makes us human.

If God is the mystery in whom this web of life has its being, then God is surely also longing to be in relationship with each of us, and with all of us.

How might this work?

Relationship is a two-way street. God wants to reveal Godself to us. We want to find a meaningful relationship with God.

Such a two-way relationship, like any human relationship, will involve some self-disclosure. God will reveal something of God's nature to us. We are invited to share ourselves and our concerns with God.

A person of faith is one who tries to read the meanings of God in our world and who desires to respond to those meanings in a way that best expresses his or her own personality.

How Could This Work?

For as long as human beings have been around on this planet, they have tried to find ways of being in relationship with God. They have discovered, for example, that God reveals Godself through the following:

- The created world
- Sacred Scripture
- The story of the universe
- The lives of people who have lived close to the heart of God
- The events of our everyday lives
- Our human relationships

Creation itself is covered with the footprints of the Creator. It shows us the delicate dance between light and darkness, action and rest, life and death. It tells us the story of how our universe began and how it is sustained, in spite of our own thoughtless lifestyles.

Sacred Scripture tells another story, of how we have tried to listen to God's voice throughout our human history. It invites us to hear God's meanings through historical accounts, through parable, through story, and through words of wisdom.

Other people show us how they have learned to relate to God and to follow where God leads, and their stories invite us to learn from them and to follow the ways of truth and love along with them.

And God is right there in our ordinary days and weeks, our conversations and interactions, our sorrows and joys, waiting to be recognized.

And Our Response?

We can begin to cultivate a relationship with God in much the same way we would with another human being.

We can share our thoughts, our fears, our joys and sorrows, our hopes and dreams, in the dialogue we call prayer. It isn't so hard.

When we express the things we feel most deeply, in the quiet of prayer, we are not really "telling God" our concerns but are bringing them to mind ourselves, in the conscious presence of God.

You could say that we are bringing them into a sharper focus, in the light of God's love, and exposing them to the beam of that love, whether we are praying for ourselves or for someone else.

We can develop this relationship by living in daily awareness of what is actually going on in our lives. We can learn to notice those moments when we feel that God is close—perhaps suggesting new directions or calming long-standing fears or opening our hearts to moments of joy in the presence of great beauty or through incidents that move us deeply.

Every movement in our hearts is an invitation to respond to God's action. Every day we live has the potential to take us a little bit further in our desire to relate to the mystery of God.

What Do You Think?

Genuine relationship, with one another or with God, depends on whether we want to be in relationship.

If the desire is there, the rest will follow.

What is your desire? In what special ways do you feel God expresses Godself to you? And how do you respond?

Every happening, great and small, is a parable whereby God speaks to us, and the art of life is to get the message.
—Malcolm Muggeridge

3
God Is Love—Could This Be True?

Albert Einstein once said that the most important question we could ever ask is, "Does the universe mean well with us?"

The question may surprise, and even shock, some Christians.

Or perhaps it is another way of asking, "Can we really believe that God is love?"

If you were to ask a random sample of people whether they think the universe is ultimately benevolent, neutral, or hostile toward us, you would probably find that the majority thinks that the universe is neutral, that it doesn't care what becomes of us.

Perhaps you feel like that yourself, especially when you think of all the problems life poses.

And yet people of faith have consistently claimed that God is love.

Is it just a cliché? Or could it possibly be true?

When we tell our children, "God loves you," do we believe it ourselves?

It's often hard to think of ourselves as being lovable at all. Maybe we haven't experienced much love in our younger lives. Maybe we have been subjected to a lot of destructive criticism. Maybe we have begun to think that we are not worth much and wonder, "Why would anyone, let alone God, love us?"

Maybe, if we are really honest, we are not totally convinced. God may be a God of love in theory, but could God possibly love me?

Two Witnesses for the Defense

God doesn't need defending, of course, any more than the ocean needs to justify itself to the fish.

But sometimes we need convincing.

What convinces me that God is love?

My first witness is my own memory bank.

There have been times in the past—maybe only a very few times, and very rare moments, but no less real and vivid ones—when I felt, with absolute clarity, the sense of God touching my life in some way.

Perhaps these were moments when I felt deeply at one with the created world or with another human being. Or moments when I felt powerfully guided in some way or profoundly comforted while in some distress.

When I recall such moments, do I feel that God's touch upon my life was a loving touch?

The answer, for me, is a resounding yes! It was always a loving touch, though frequently also a very challenging touch.

My second witness is Jesus of Nazareth, whom Christians believe to be a unique manifestation of God in human form.

How did Jesus touch the lives of those around him? Was it with love, or was it neutral, or even hostile?

I don't think even the fiercest detractors of Christianity would suggest that Jesus' actions were ever neutral!

No! Jesus went about his world touching people with healing, with life, with new hope, and with compassion, although that touch was often very challenging.

Love from Day 1?

Scientists tell us that at the very beginning of our universe, there was a slight imbalance between particles and antiparticles. We don't need to know what particles and antiparticles are to understand that this tiny imbalance led to the possibility of life. The fact is that when a particle meets an antiparticle, they mutually destroy each other. Had there been no imbalance, there would have been no universe, no Earth, no you or me. The imbalance was minute, but it was in favor of the particles. Those particles that survived eventually became the primeval components of life.

I would call that a universe that actively desires life.

I would call that a God who is striving, constantly, even from Day 1, to bring forth life in all its fullness.

And there are a host of other examples in science where a tiny imbalance in favor of what leads to life made all the difference.

So, I believe . . . that at the heart of all that is, is a mystery I call God, and that this mystery is intentional. Its intention is always to bring forth the more life-giving outcome, in the story of creation just as in the story of each one of us.

It is a loving intention, and a personal intention.

And therefore, although God is clearly not a person like us but bigger and better, God is a personal power, with an overwhelmingly loving intention toward all creation and to each creature, including even me.

What Do You Think?

What evidence do you find in your own life that God's touch is a touch of love?

When you say, "God is love," can you believe it?

> *I am a little pencil in the hand of a writing God who is sending a love letter to the world.*
> —Blessed Teresa of Calcutta

4

Certainty or Mystery?

Alice in *Alice in Wonderland* complains about the demand on her to believe "six impossible things before breakfast." For many people the process of initiation into a religious tradition might feel rather like this. Candidates for baptism or confirmation, for example, might be required to undergo some significant period of instruction about the doctrinal propositions to which they will be required to assent.

In some cultures this instruction begins with the very young and takes the form of a "catechism" of the tenets of the faith, which they will learn by heart, not always with any degree of real understanding. More recently, however, this process has often been superseded by a more enlightened guided journey of discovery into what the life of faith might mean within a particular tradition.

This change highlights the challenging questions: "Am I yearning for certainty, or am I open to the risk of mystery? Do I see faith as a set of absolute beliefs with which I can agree, or is faith for me more like a journey of discovery, drawing me constantly beyond all my limited certainties and toward a mystery that will always lie beyond my understanding?"

A related question might be, "If I align myself to a faith community, am I joining a members-only organization, or do I see myself rather as part of an adventure that welcomes every searching heart?"

Some Thoughts to Ponder

We often hear that religion causes much of the world's conflicts. If this is so, why might that be?

You may have heard about the three people who claimed to have seen God. They began to argue about how God looked and what God was wearing—and especially about the color of God's hat. One swore that it was a red hat. The other had seen a yellow hat. The third was totally convinced that God's hat was blue. What none of them realized was that God's hat was a rainbow hat, with a different color shining out from every angle.

If they had been able to sit more lightly with their imagined certainties, they might have avoided conflict and in fact come to learn a lot from one another, which would have enriched them all.

Of course, the color of God's hat is a trivial fiction.

Our certainties become much more damaging when we convince ourselves that certain tenets about faith are absolute and then try to impose them on others, who will have a different set of "certainties." It isn't hard to see where this kind of fundamentalism is leading us.

Certainty divides us. Mystery unites us.

A Cautionary Tale

I was once sitting in a little park in the small town of Loyola in Spain. Behind me was the imposing basilica of St. Ignatius, who was born there. Its edifice at that time was covered in scaffolding and under renovation. In front of me was a small kiosk selling newspapers, chocolate, and other small items.

A man came along with his small daughter and their dog. The man bought a newspaper for himself and a little container of soap bubbles for his daughter to play with. They sat down beside me. The man was engrossed in his newspaper. The little girl was delightedly blowing bubbles, clearly entranced by the magical colored globe that each bubble formed as it caught the sunlight. The dog jumped up after every bubble and tried to catch it, but as soon as he seized the bubble with his snout, the bubble burst.

I asked myself, "Which is teaching me more about the kingdom of God—the mighty basilica with all its scaffolding or this little girl's joy at the beauty of the world reflected in her bubbles?" The little dog was a reminder that as soon as we try to take hold of the mystery and pin it down into our own categories, words, and meanings, we destroy it.

If we think we have "got" it, we will lose it.

If we think we have "arrived," we have gone down a cul-de-sac.

What Do You Think?

The idea of God will always lie beyond the grasp of limited, time-bound human minds. God will always be a mystery. If the reality we call God were not a mystery, it would not be God.

How do you feel about living and growing within this mystery that will defy all your attempts to fit it into human categories?

True faith [is] a leap away from fossilised beliefs
into the mystery of the Unknown God.
—Søren Kierkegaard

5

Does Life Have Any Meaning?

There is a big divide between people who regard life as a random event in a random universe, with no inherent meaning, and those who believe that their life's journey, and the journey of all humanity, has real meaning and purpose.

Perhaps there is no answer.

But to be a person of faith is to come down on the side of meaning.

And our deep desire to discover meaning in life might in itself be a sign that there is meaning to be discovered.

Most religions are attempts to formulate the meaning of life in terms of a particular understanding of God. But do those formulations really satisfy our heart's searching? To be truly convinced that life has meaning and purpose, perhaps we need to search our own experience first, because any sense of purpose will be personal before it becomes universal.

In today's world, it is easy to despair of any progress in our human journey. The news headlines emphasize the opposite kind of movement—a regression rather than a progression, and the return of chaos rather than growth toward a higher and more compassionate order.

So which is right, the voice of despair or the voice of hope? Resignation to the apparent disintegration of society or the desire to turn things in a different direction?

So What Is It All About?

A friend sent me a humorous greeting card with the caption: "What if the hokey pokey really *is* what it's all about?"

Fair question. But the same friend who sent the card spends her life unstintingly, caring for young children. Her life has meaning. More than the hokey pokey, I would suggest.

So what could the purpose of our existence really be?

Everyone would have a different answer, and certainly no one would have the definitive answer.

But our desires give us some clues.

On New Year's Eve in 1999, television around the globe followed the dawn of the new millennium through all the world's time zones, and everywhere the hopes and dreams people expressed were the same: peace. Not just the absence of conflict, but the deep wholeness of things expressed in the Hebrew word *shalom*.

Could this be an indication of life's meaning? To become, individually and collectively, the best that we can be? To build a society in which everyone can live in freedom and peace? To evolve over time into higher levels of consciousness, where compassion would prevail over egotism and cooperation over competition? In short, the kind of world for which Jesus himself lived, and died?

What Is My Role in the Journey?

A traveler once went into a little shop. The shopkeeper asked, "What would you like? We have everything here that you could desire."

The traveler's reply came promptly. "I would like a world where all can live in peace, where everyone has enough to eat and every child can go to school. I want a world where everyone looks out for their neighbor and cares for others as much as for their own kith and kin."

At this point the shopkeeper interrupted: "Sorry sir. I forgot to mention: we don't sell the fruits here; we only sell the seeds."

If we believe that life has meaning and purpose, we can make our dreams a reality. We can, and must, become the change we want to see.

Change won't happen on its own. It won't grow unless we plant the seeds.

So our role is very clear. As people of faith, we believe that each of us carries a seed of God's kingdom—

something that only we can plant and nurture, each of us uniquely.

The challenge is to recognize the particular way in which we can personally help nudge the human family a little bit closer to God's dream for *shalom*.

If we believe that we are part of a journey that has meaning and purpose, how are we going to make that journey a reality?

What Do You Think?

Is there a reason you are here?

What kind of special seed can your life sow into the field of human growth? How are you going to nourish it?

Tell me, what is it you plan to do with your one wild and precious life?
—Mary Oliver

Let us endeavor so to live that when we come to die even the undertaker will be sorry.
—Mark Twain

6
What Is My Life's Center?

Only a few hundred years ago, most people were completely convinced that the sun revolved around planet Earth and that our planet was the center of the entire universe. And since they also thought human beings were the pinnacle and ultimate purpose of creation on the earth, it followed that humankind was at the center of the universe and therefore free to exploit creation as we wished.

Today, with the benefit of all our technology and our increasing understanding of the origins of our universe, we flinch at such arrogance. And yet we tend to live our daily lives as though nothing has changed—as though human needs always take precedence over the needs of our planet and as though our personal desires or those of our family or our tribe go ahead of the needs of the rest of creation.

The result of this kind of thinking is obvious: rivalry, mutual distrust, conflict, and war—the very opposite of the deep human longing for *shalom*. The center of gravity lies in ourselves and our egos, and everything else has to come into orbit around that ego center.

The truth is, creation's center of gravity lies much deeper than in any individual need or requirement. The universe revolves around the balance of life itself. For this balance to be maintained, every living thing has to live in harmony with that reality or else be in perpetual conflict.

A Different Way

But there is another way. The people we most revere in the human story are usually those who have chosen to walk to the beat of a different drum, challenging us to find less egocentric ways of relating to God and to one another.

We rate altruism high on the scale of human values, and we deplore selfishness. This way of seeing things finds expression in the spiritual precept, found in different forms of words in most religious traditions, that we often call the Golden Rule: Love your neighbor as you love yourself. Behave toward others in the way you would wish them to behave toward you.

We sense intuitively, and we try to teach our children, that we should put the greater good before our own personal benefit, but the ego fights back—hard! We can find ourselves swimming against the currents of a me-first society and the attitudes of our contemporary culture. We also find it surprisingly hard to love ourselves, as the Golden Rule calls us to do. If we are unkind to ourselves, we have no chance of being truly compassionate toward others.

To be a person of faith is to make a choice to center one's life around the deeper center of gravity we call God, and the greater good of all creation, rather than primarily around one's personal gain and benefit. It is to act with lovingkindness, to ourselves and to one another.

How Can We Do This in Practice?

It sounds easy and obvious, but in practice it is very difficult to maintain this deeper focus.

One problem we have in turning the ideal into the real is that we try to leap across miles rather than navigate inches. We are asked not to save the world but only to take each next step with regard for this deeper center that holds us in balance with the Golden Rule.

A helpful and practical way to do this is by using a kind of reflective prayer, often called the Review, or the *examen*.

Take a short time, ten to fifteen minutes, ideally each day, to play back what has actually happened during the day, how you felt about it, and how you reacted. Ask yourself: "What happened today to make me feel more alive, more truly myself, more grounded in the core of my being? What happened today for which I want to say, 'Thank you'? Did I do or say anything today for which I feel regret?"

Notice especially any memories that cause a strong reaction in you—perhaps joy or gratitude, or anger, regret, or some kind of inner disturbance. These "hot spots" are indicators that these parts of your day's experience are important and have something to show you about the deepest movements of your heart. Remember the image of the fish swimming in the mystery of the ocean: these movements are like the currents in the ocean, helping you navigate a true course, in right relationship with yourself, with others, with all of creation, and with God.

What Do You Think?

You have probably made a deep and lifelong commitment to try to live from your own deepest center in God, when you committed yourself to a life of faith. However, there will be moments every day when you temporarily turn away from this deep commitment in pursuit of your more ego-centered interests.

Try using the Review prayer to check out those turnings and re-turnings, and notice their root causes in your own lived experience.

Make a note of any parts of that experience where you feel you tend to follow the ego and any parts that tend to be more deeply grounded in your true center, where God is indwelling.

Everyone must decide whether to walk in the light of creative altruism or in the darkness of destructive selfishness.
—Martin Luther King Jr.

7
Who Is Jesus?

Two thousand years ago, in a remote village in the Middle East, a child was born who was destined to turn the world around.

Plenty of people have tried to define who he was and uncover the nature of his personhood. There is no shortage of doctrines surrounding the question of who we think he was and is.

Faith tells me that this man is the person I need to follow, the person who for me reveals everything that humanity is called to become—everything that God is dreaming we can become. He shows us what our humanity can look like when it is fully evolved. He also shows us the cost of following the path that leads us to this fulfillment of who we are.

Faith tells me this. Simple faith tells me that if I truly want to follow him, I don't need to get tangled up in all the (sometimes conflicting) theories and doctrines about him.

All kinds of different people were attracted to Jesus' teaching when he lived on the earth. Many were simple, illiterate peasants who apparently had no problem understanding him and responding to him. Others were highly educated people. Some were models of good behavior, exemplary in their religious practice. Others were a mess, and they knew it. It clearly didn't require a doctorate in theology to follow this man. In fact too much head learning, and certainly too much "righteousness," appears to have been more hindrance than help along the way.

What Can We Say about Him?

We know some basic facts about Jesus from independent historical accounts from the time of his earthly lifetime.

That he lived in what today is Israel and was executed for alleged sedition are historical facts beyond reasonable dispute.

But Christians believe a lot more about him than these bare facts.

We believe that he shows us, in a unique way, what the fullness of God's love is like when it takes human form.

We believe that he incarnates the Word that underpins all creation and the Light that reveals not only the divine glory but also the depth of our shadows.

We believe that he shows us not only the goal of our human journey but also the cost of its fulfillment.

We believe that he shows us through his teachings and his life what it means to live by a completely different set of values from those that normally prevail in our societies and personal lives.

We believe that when he died, his essential spirit was released in a way that liberated the pure energy of God in what we call the Holy Spirit and that this energy empowers us to follow Jesus in our own living. Because of this, we believe that Jesus has truly transcended what our human understanding sees as death.

The Heart of the Matter

It's impossible to know for sure exactly what Jesus said and did during his life on the earth. But we do have four accounts of his life, death, and resurrection in the four Gospels that were selected to be included in our New Testament Scriptures.

At the very heart of these accounts is the astonishing challenge of what we call the Beatitudes. These blessings of Jesus to his followers turn all our expectations on their heads. They tell us, in different ways, that those who appear to have nothing, those in grief, those in poverty, those who are maligned and persecuted, those who are meek and gentle, are closest to the real core of what it means to be truly human. Only when we have nothing left to lose can we discover the core of who we really are. Only when we allow God to upturn our self-focused values will we see where our true destiny is leading us.

Such teaching might well fill us with fear. How can we possibly live like that? Jesus' answer is clear, and frequently repeated: "Don't be afraid!"

He doesn't just say it or preach it or teach it. He lives it, by living totally true to God's dream, regardless of the cost. He dies it, freely allowing the powers of darkness to destroy him. And then he transcends it, releasing the power of his whole being to flow through all those who follow after him.

Who Is Jesus for You?

Jesus once asked his friends the question, "Who do you say that I am?" (Matthew 16:15).

If he were to ask you this question, how would you respond?

Jesus is God spelling Himself out in language that man can understand.
—S. D. Gordon

He changed sunset into sunrise.
—St. Clement of Alexandria

8
Following Jesus

The Invitation

Again and again in the Gospels, Jesus issues the invitation "Follow me." He doesn't say, "Worship me." He doesn't say, "Go to church." He says, "Follow me," "Trust me," and over and over, "Don't be afraid."

When John's disciples ask him, "Where do you live? What are you about? What makes you tick?" he gives not an answer but an invitation: "Come and see" (see John 1:39). He invites us to make a journey of discovery—about who we are and can become, who our "neighbor" is, who Jesus is, and who God is for us.

To follow Jesus is to hear and respond to this invitation, to follow, to come and see for ourselves who he is for us and what his presence in our hearts is asking of us in our world today.

Sometimes that "follow me" is a daunting challenge. For example, he invites people to leave behind what they have been doing so far, or at least to leave behind their familiar methods. He invites us to let go of old securities, even an old way of life, and to set out on a road that has no signposts but only a traveling companion who is waiting to accompany and guide us step-by-step.

Because it *is* so challenging and frightening, Jesus urges his companions, time and time again, not to be afraid. Fear is our worst enemy when it comes to responding to this invitation to become "people of the Way." Jesus takes the fear head-on and leads us beyond it, if we dare to follow.

The Way

So, what is this Way we are invited to walk?

It is the Way of Love. Jesus tells us not only to love our neighbor but also to love our enemies and, maybe hardest of all, to love ourselves. How do we generate this love when perhaps we don't feel loving at all? I find the words of the author M. Scott Peck very helpful here. He reminds us, "Love is not an emotion. Love is a decision." So what Jesus is asking of us is not to feel loving toward everyone we meet but to choose freely to do the most loving, the most life-giving, thing in every situation. This puts a rather different slant on it. The impossible becomes a little bit more possible. We can't control how we feel, but we can choose how we act and what we say in every situation. We can choose our attitude toward the people we meet. We can choose generosity over spitefulness, an encouraging word over a sarcastic remark.

It is the Way of Truth. Jesus asks us, in every situation, to act and speak in a way that rings true at the core of our being—to do the right thing, not in hope of any reward or for fear of any punishment but simply because it is the right thing, the more loving thing, to do. He doesn't just ask this of us; he shows us in every action and choice of his own life what it looks like to live completely true to the core of our soul, where God is indwelling. He calls us to do as he does and take into ourselves the values and attitudes that his own life reveals, seeking to make them our own.

It is the Way of Life. If we dare to walk this Way, we will discover that it leads to "life in all its fullness." It invites us to become human beings fully alive.

The Cost

When you live true to the very best in yourself, perhaps by speaking out against injustice or stating your truth in a hostile situation, you will provoke a reaction. For example, so-called whistle-blowers who expose wrongdoing in their own profession are likely to be ostracized by their fellow professionals and may even be excluded from practicing their profession. Even a small remark that challenges unacceptable behavior can elicit a very violent response.

Jesus is the one who lives completely true to the Father's dream for humanity. He shines like a light in the darkness. But that light provokes the darkness, and the darkness rises up to swallow and apparently destroy him. He is executed because he is a constant threat to national security and a thorn in the flesh of the religious authorities. He warns his followers that they, too, will be crucified in some form if they live true to his teachings. If you have ever spoken out about some issue in your own situations, including religious issues, you will have experienced something of what it means to "take up your cross" and follow him.

Jesus knows very well what the consequences will be for those who follow him and live true to his words, but he doesn't just tell us not to be afraid. He says to us: "Follow me, and the darkness will seek to overwhelm you too, but *trust* me: I am going to live true to God, and let the darkness destroy me, and then I am going to transcend the worst that the darkness can ever do. I am with you and in you through that journey of the cross, and with me you, too, will transcend the power of death."

What Do You Think?

The invitation is given again and again, to each of us, every day.

The Way is waiting to welcome us.

The cost is high.

How do you choose to respond?

I am the way, and the truth, and the life.
—John 14:6

9
Entering the Gospels
in Prayer

If following Jesus really means trying to take his values and attitudes as the guide for our own choices and actions, if it means choosing to do the more loving, the more life-giving, the more Christlike thing in every situation, however we might feel about it, then we are left with the problematic question of how would we know what this more Christlike choice would be.

We can ask, "What would Jesus do here?" but the difficulty with this is our enormous capacity to delude ourselves, and when we ask, "What would Jesus do?" or even "What is God's will?" we are likely to convince ourselves that God would want pretty much what we were planning anyway. There is a better way to open ourselves to what the mind and heart of Christ would suggest in a particular situation: spend time praying with the Gospels.

There are two time-honored methods of doing this, which we will explore here. But whichever method you use, remember that what we ask in this form of prayer is not "What happened, to whom, and how?" or "What did Jesus say or do at this point?" These questions are interesting, but we address them primarily in our head and with our intellect. They are the very valid subjects of Bible study, but in scriptural prayer we ask rather, "What does this story mean to me, and how does it connect to the events and situations in my own life right now? What does it reveal about the attitude Jesus would demonstrate in such a situation, and what values would shape his choices?"

Imaginative Meditation

Your imagination can be a wonderful ally in scriptural prayer. Some people distrust their imagination and can't believe it could bring them closer to God. Yet how often did Jesus say, "Imagine you are tending your sheep, baking your bread . . . Let me show you how these very things tell you what the kingdom of God is like"?

When you desire to enter into the Gospel narratives and meet God there, try choosing a passage—perhaps a healing miracle or a parable—and letting your imagination take you to the scene. Notice what picture comes to mind, without trying to manufacture it. Notice who is there and where you are. If you feel drawn to do so, converse with others at the scene, the disciples, the crowd, and especially with Jesus. What do you want to say? What do you feel

Jesus might want to say to you? Does this scene have any connection to what is going on in your life? Does this passage show you anything about where Jesus would stand in the situation you are reflecting on?

Don't make any judgments, either about yourself or about others. Just notice what happens and how you feel, and let those responses rest in the stillness of your prayer. After your time of prayer is over, take a moment to reflect on the experience, and maybe even make a note in a journal of what you feel this prayer has been about for you. How are you going to move on in this situation in light of this prayer? Is there anything further you would want to express to God now, after your time of reflection?

Lectio divina

Another ancient method of scriptural prayer is called *lectio divina*, which involves reading a short passage of Scripture; noticing whether any word, phrase, or image especially speaks to you; taking time to meditate on what that fragment means to you; and then letting what you have noticed turn into action. To use this method in your everyday life, try the following process:

1. Begin the day by reading a passage of Scripture (using any method you prefer: part of the day's reading if you belong to a lectionary-based denomination or perhaps a daily Bible reading guide, or just simply choose a passage at random).

2. Notice whether any phrase, word, image, or thought leaps out at you and engages your mind.

3. Reflect on that small fragment as you go through the day. Whenever you have a spare moment (when you are stuck in traffic or taking a shower or walking the dog or taking a coffee break), bring it to mind and let it soak deeper into your heart, asking the question, "What does this passage mean for me today and how does it relate to my life situations?"

4. At the end of the day, take a few minutes to reflect on the fruits of your prayer and bring your response to God in whatever way feels right for you.

Could This Work for You?

Praying with Scripture in these or other ways can help shape our daily living in surprisingly powerful ways. We think we are trying to "get inside" the Scriptures, but what is actually happening is that the Scriptures are getting inside us and gradually shaping our attitudes and values so that they come closer to the mind and heart of Jesus. Try it for yourself, and remember the importance of reflecting on your experience, perhaps by keeping a journal or by sharing something of your prayer journey with a trusted friend.

An unexamined life is not worth living.
—Socrates

10
Can My Life Make Any Difference?

I was once traveling home on a Sunday in a train full of students returning to college after a weekend at home. One of them, sitting right next to me, was doing an assignment. She had been asked to think of what mattered to her in her choice of a career. She had lots of points, including job satisfaction, using her gifts, and earning a good salary. But right at the top of her list, and way ahead of other considerations was the statement of desire:

"I want to make a difference."

We all want to make a difference. Most people hope that when their lives are over, they will be leaving the world a slightly better place than it was when they arrived.

And just as surely, most of us don't really believe our lives can make a difference. We think we are too small to count, too insignificant to have any impact on the big scheme of things, too unimportant for our tiny voices to be heard.

Are we just kidding ourselves with our thoughts of changing the world?

"What can I do?" we ask ourselves resignedly, in the face of gross injustice or the horror of other people's suffering.

But what if . . . *faith makes a difference?*

What if that were true? What if each one of us matters—really matters?

A Few Thoughts to Ponder

This whole universe, with its trillions of galaxies, began as a tiny speck of concentrated energy, smaller than a grain of salt.

When you were first conceived, you were just a single cell, a mere pinpoint of life, barely visible to the naked eye but packed full of the potential for everything you would ever become—every action, choice, and relationship.

You are just a drop in the ocean, but without you the ocean will not become the ocean.

You are just a grain of sand, but you are a grain of sand that tips the scales.

You are just a drop of dew that soaks into the earth and is gone by noon, but that drop of dew brings life to the seed that grows in the earth.

You are only one, but the Power of One is greater than you dare to dream.

One is not Nothing. One makes a difference.

Your choices can tip the scales of humanity a little bit more toward goodness and truth, if that is your desire.

But How?

To be a person of faith is to believe that you can make a difference and to work at making that happen.

It's about turning the ideal into the real. And we get to do that in the small things that happen every day.

We have a choice about those thoughtless comments, destructive put-downs, sarcastic rejoinders, times when we walk past a needy neighbor without offering help, times when we say nothing to challenge an injustice.

These things happen every day, and they are in our own power to change.

Just as surely, we can choose to offer an encouraging comment when we might have said nothing, to give time and a listening ear when someone close to us is hurting, to take some small step to do what we can—to slow climate change, to live more simply, to speak a word of tolerance and understanding where there is strife. There are opportunities for these things every day, and they are ours to use or not to use.

The currency of change is in our own back pockets.

A person of faith is one who chooses to spend that currency, moment by moment, by making ordinary choices that tip the scales toward the greater good.

What Do You Think?

Do you want to make a difference?

Do you believe you can?

Take time to notice the choices you actually make today, the ways you choose to react to others, the words you choose to say. This is the currency of change. How do you feel about how you want to spend it?

> *Ideals are like stars.*
> *You can never reach them.*
> *But you can use them to help you plot your*
> *course.*
> —André Gide

11
Faith Is as Faith Does

Imagine this scene: John the Baptist, Jesus' friend and kinsman, is in prison because he has fallen afoul of the authorities. From his prison cell he hears about all that Jesus is doing, and he wonders, "Is this man really the promised Messiah, or are we still waiting for another to appear?" He sends out his own disciples to ask Jesus face-to-face. The answer comes back, not a simple yes or no, but this: go back and tell John what you have seen—blind people seeing again, lame people walking, people with contagious disease being cleansed, the deaf hearing again and the dead being raised to new life, and above all, the poorest of the poor are being given good news, that they are worth everything in God's eyes and are sure of God's special blessing and care (Matthew 11:2–5).

This incident reminds me of a sermon I once heard in an urban church in a poor part of town. The preacher asked, "Suppose a stranger were to come to you today and stop you in the street, and ask you, 'Where might I find Jesus of Nazareth? What would you say?'" There were a few murmured suggestions from among the congregation. Some would send the seeker to the nearest church, or maybe even the cathedral.

The preacher went on. "Yes, of course you might find him in a church, but maybe no more and no less there than anywhere else. What about the local hospital, where dedicated medical staff are tending the same people Jesus once tended? What about the schools, where devoted teachers are nurturing young minds? What about those who are working to get a fairer deal for the poorest among us? And what about the ordinary homes along your street, where men and women are looking out for their neighbors and caring for their children and elderly relatives?"

Where Do You See These Things Happening?

Jesus invites John to decide for himself who Jesus is, not on the basis of what people say they believe about him but on the basis of the effects he has, because of what he is doing. If you want to know what kind of a tree is in front of you, look at its fruits, not its botanical name. If you want to know where Jesus is now, look around you, not at the statements of a creed but at the ways in which his Spirit is working in our lives today.

Faith is as faith does. To profess faith in Jesus and in the God he calls Abba is to allow that Spirit to flow through our own lives and prompt and guide us to be present for others in the way that Jesus models for us. We may not personally have the power to cure the sick, to give sight to the blind or hearing to the deaf (although some do), but we are asked, in every situation we encounter, to choose to do the more loving, the more life-giving, the more Christ-like thing next, in what we say and what we do.

Living like this is a great deal more demanding than merely affirming with our lips that we believe certain things about God and about Jesus, who incarnates the spirit of God in human form. It is easy to say a lot and do nothing. It is possible to do a great deal, and yet not say or assert anything. People of faith live as though they mean what they say they believe, and they strive to be more like the one they claim to follow.

Turning Contemplation into Action

I have a little oil lamp that a friend gave me, and it's a constant reminder to me that a life of faith involves both contemplation and action.

The oil lamp has a wick, and the wick has two ends. If there is to be light, then one end of the wick has to remain submerged in the oil, and the other end has to extend into the world. Only then is it possible for a flame to bring both warmth and light.

A person of faith is one who is called to bring a bit more light and warmth into the world. To do this, we must remain rooted in a life of prayer and reflection, finding God in the ordinary things around us and immersing ourselves from time to time in the deep silence of our hearts, where God is indwelling. But it is also necessary to be "out there," burning with love and compassion, justice and peace, in a world that longs for light in its darkness and new ways forward through the maze of contemporary life. If either of these is lacking, then our lives will not be channels of God's warmth and light.

As you look around, where do you see fruits of the "Jesus tree" budding and sprouting?

Where do you see joy shining in the world?

Where do you see actions motivated by love?

Where would you direct someone who comes looking for the spirit of Jesus of Nazareth in your neighborhood?

How would you feel if someone were to direct such a person to your door?

How is the wick in your oil lamp?

Just a Question

Life and love are for spending, not for saving. On what, or on whom, will you choose to spend yours?

> *Not everyone who says to me, "Lord, Lord," will enter the kingdom of heaven, but only one who does the will of my Father in heaven.*
> —Matthew 7:21

> *Love ought to show itself in deeds over and above words.*
> —St. Ignatius Loyola, *The Spiritual Exercises*

12

Journeying Alone, Journeying Together

Getting the right balance between solitude and community is always going to be a challenge as we journey in faith.

For some people, often those of a more introverted disposition, the tendency will be to see faith as something private and solitary, shaped by personal prayer and personal choices about how to live a God-centered life in the real world. The danger in this approach is that we may come to regard faith as a means of obtaining an individual passport to heaven.

For others, often the more extroverted of temperament, faith will be seen more as a community matter, expressed through public worship and in the embrace of an identifiable faith community, or church. The danger in this position is that public religious observance may lead to our neglecting the need for individual prayer and reflection.

Both understandings are true, and both dangers are real. Jesus warns us that the way of discipleship is narrow, and to some extent, we will have to walk it in single file. This means that we are invited to relate to God through personal prayer, which, by definition, is something we make in solitude.

However, the fruits of that prayer will affect not only us but also those around us, and indeed, the world as a whole. We are not independent beings but interdependent beings, each a unique node in the vast web of life, and each affecting every other part of that web through what we say and do and how we make our choices. So faith is the journey of a single soul but also a community matter.

The Faith Community

Like-minded people will always gather to share something of their lives with one another. This is especially true when it comes to questions of faith. A faith community is a group of people who gather regularly to express their faith in particular forms that they find helpful. This is traditionally known as going to church, but that's a misnomer, because church isn't a place we go to but a community of people we *are*, and this is as true in the streets as it is in the cathedral, as true on Monday as it is on Sunday.

Churchgoing is not necessarily the same thing as living a life of faith. It is possible to go to church services every week, or even every day, and still miss the point of what it means to follow Jesus. And it is possible to follow Jesus without going to church. Nevertheless, a faith community in some form is, I would suggest, an indispensable part of what it means to make a journey in faith.

We must discover for ourselves where, and with whom, our faith community is to be found. For many it will be the traditional forms of church or chapel, but an increasing number of people who are trying to follow Jesus and live their lives in alignment with his values and teaching are exploring other forms of building community that will nourish and guide them on this quest.

It really doesn't matter what we call our faith communities, or how they are organized, or where they meet. What matters is that we understand that we, as human beings, are born for community and that we have real meaning as individuals only when we are in relationship—*right* relationship—with others.

Soul Friends

Our Celtic forebears, who founded Christian communities in Ireland and the British Isles, honored a role they called the *anam cara*, which means "soul friend." A soul friend is a person you trust enough to share some of the deepest matters of your heart, someone who will listen to what you share without any kind of judgment, without trying to "fix" anything, and without flattering or criticizing you. He or she will, however, listen lovingly to whatever you share and then perhaps reflect back what seems to be stirring you most deeply, possibly also challenging you in firm but gentle ways—for example, reminding you of what you have consistently been desiring or discerning in your prayer and in your life, warning you if it appears that you are being untrue to your own deepest longings and intentions.

Soul friends are a bit like midwives. They help bring Christ to birth in your life and circumstances, but they only assist at the birth. They don't second-guess what form the baby will take, and they let the birth happen in its own way and time. They are there not to administer medication to take away the pain but to be alongside you as you deal with it. It is you who does the laboring, but they will rejoice with you at the miracle that is coming to pass.

How do you find a soul friend? Look around you. Seek and you will find, and perhaps in places you didn't expect. A soul friend is someone your soul can connect to and your heart can trust. It isn't necessarily someone with a string of qualifications. One of the wisest soul friends I know is a woman who left school at fourteen and sees herself as a humble housewife, mother, and grandmother.

What about You?

What does "faith community" mean to you, and where do you find yours?

Do you have anyone you would see as a soul friend? If not, is this a relationship you would like to consider seeking out?

Perhaps others already see you as a soul friend on their journey. How would you feel about that? Is there anything you could do to improve your listening skills?

> *Christ says [in Matthew 18:20] "Wherever two or more are gathered in my name there I am." To be gathered in his name is to see beyond the illusion of the separate self and realize that, deep down, we are not separate but actually interdependent and inter-connected.*
> —Paul Levi

13
I Want to Ask God . . .

. . . Why Bad Things Happen

It's the perennial question: if there is a God, why do catastrophes happen, and why do bad things strike the good as well as the sinners? The old saying catches the problem: "The rain it falleth on the just and on the unjust fella, but it falleth more upon the just, 'cause the unjust has the just's umbrella."

Not only do calamities strike indiscriminately, but law-abiding and peaceable people seem to get it twice over, once at the hands of fortune and again at the hands of their more unscrupulous neighbors.

But we inhabit a living planet. A planet without earthquakes, tsunamis, and hurricanes would be inert. Life would certainly not have evolved on it. Change and upheaval go with the territory. Just as a child is not born into the world without labor and agony on the part of the mother, so life on this earth comes into being through great contractions of the natural order—and those contractions often bring devastation in their wake.

It's a different matter when we do harm to one another or collude with systems that thrive on war and exploitation. The question is then not why God allows it, but why we do it and what we are going to do about it. In his book *When Bad Things Happen to Good People*, Harold Kushner suggests that while our usual question is, "God, why is this happening to me?" a more helpful question for a person of faith might be, "God, this is happening to me. Now, how are you and I together going to deal with it in the most life-giving way, so that we can move on?"

. . . About Sin and Eternal Punishment

The Aramaic language, I understand, often has many layers of meaning, which we tend to translate into just one or a few words in English, thereby missing the depth of significance that Jesus, as an Aramaic speaker, would have understood and intended.

A classic example is the word *sin*, just one word to signify a great many layers of possible meaning. One of these is the reality that we often experience of missing the mark, of not getting things right, of compromising on our best, of failing to focus on what really matters.

Another layer of meaning is "unripeness." What if sin is like being an unripe fruit, bitter and unpalatable compared to how it should be when it is fully ripe—or like a fractious child, who is only just learning the ways of being a social and un-self-centered human being? What if humanity as a whole is still very unripe, still just teenagers in the scheme of things, or even terrible two-year-olds?

As to eternal punishment, much of our sense of it has come down to us through tradition. I once visited Yellowstone National Park in Wyoming with a friend. We saw sulfur lakes there, belching forth reeking fumes and looking like something out of Dante's *Inferno*. We gazed down on them in horror. I asked my friend, "Can you imagine being here with someone who has done something really bad to you, and then picking them up and hurling them down into *that*?" "No way," she replied, grimacing in horror.

If she wouldn't, and I wouldn't, and you wouldn't, why do we think that God *would*?

. . . Why Jesus Had to Die

The question of why Jesus had to die is the arena of much debate and disagreement. A teenager once said to me, "I know I don't always do things right, I can be selfish and mean, but even so, they're not pinning this man's death on *me*." I had to concede that she was right and that, if we stop to think about it, we would be hard-pressed to say just how our misdemeanors, or even our fundamental lack of integrity, really caused God to hand over Jesus to the horror of crucifixion and whether we really believe that. Many ask, "What kind of God would that be?" Surely the same kind of God we used to think was waiting to throw us into the sulfur lakes for any infringement of the rules.

During his lifetime, Jesus took on the forces of oppression and domination of his time, both secular and ecclesiastical, and exposed their hypocrisy and their bankruptcy. Those forces then didn't appreciate people speaking up for peace and justice any more than they do now. Today, if you speak up loudly and insistently enough, you will almost certainly be silenced, and sometimes that silencing is brutal and violent.

One way of looking at why Jesus had to die is this: in his lifetime he lived absolutely true to God's dream and God's values. He shone like a bright beam of light in a dark place, and the darkness didn't like it. He provoked the shadow side of humanity, and the shadow fought back by engulfing him and apparently destroying him. He constantly urged people: "Live true to God and to yourself in every situation. The darkness may seek to destroy you, but I will show you that the worst that can happen can never destroy the spirit of who you are. I am living this truth, and I will die for it, and then I will transcend that destruction, and my spirit will flow free forever." Trust me, follow me, and don't be afraid.

What Would You Like to Ask God?

We would all like to ask God questions, and we would all bring a different set of questions to the table. We have touched on just three such questions. There are many, many more. But are there really any answers?

Try naming your questions to yourself, and then perhaps sharing them with other trusted soul friends and listening to their questions.

So, what is faith?

Perhaps faith is not to know but still to trust.

> *Have patience with everything unresolved in your heart and try to love the questions themselves as if they were locked rooms or books written in a very foreign language. Don't search for the answers, which could not be given to you now, because you would not be able to live them. And the point is to live everything. Live the questions now. Perhaps then, someday far in the future, you will gradually, without even noticing it, live your way into the answer.*
> —Rainer Maria Rilke, *Letters to a Young Poet*

14
I Need to Ask Myself . . .

. . . What Really Matters Most to Me?

I once met a young financial adviser who seemed to have his feet firmly on the ladder to success—until his life fell apart when his marriage ended. He had to move into a small rented apartment. Most of his savings were consumed by an acrimonious divorce settlement. And he got to see his beloved two children only on alternate weekends.

What he said to me in the course of our brief conversation made a deep impression on me. Here was a young man with everything to strive for, and this is how he summed up the lessons of his recent past: "I have learned so much in this past year. I used to think I wanted a bigger house, expensive holidays, a fast car, and I told myself I wanted these as much for the family as for myself. Now I have come to understand that there are only two questions in life that really matter: How will I spend my time, and who with?"

I think that says in a sentence what people have written whole books about. Life is about how we spend the precious gift of the time we have been given, and it's about the relationships we make as we live that life.

Perhaps a life of faith is about choosing to spend our lives not just for ourselves but for the greater good, and about letting all our relationships be centered on our core relationship with God.

. . . Am I Trying to Spend My Life or Save It?

All small children go through the "my" and "mine" stage. When they see something they want, they claim it as "mine" and vigorously defend their right to it. They look at you in disbelief if you point out that nothing is actually "mine" or "ours" or "theirs," but that everything is gift. Most of us will learn the truth of this, but some people, of course, never do grow out of the "my" stage. They continue to believe that the good things in life are for claiming and owning, and that spiritual salvation itself can become a prize to win and be stored away.

Traditional religious practice can sometimes foster this desire to be "saved," to get the coveted passport to heaven, to get our ticket for the celestial banquet and be counted among God's favored ones. There is a temptation to regard God's favor as a stock market investment that we hope will pay the right dividends when the time comes.

But Jesus' life is spent, not saved. He shows us throughout his ministry and teaching that we are to give ourselves away, not hoard ourselves and our gifts and resources.

There is a Christmas story of the "fourth wise man," who set out with the others, carrying his gift to bring to the Christ child, but as he journeyed he kept meeting people who were in desperate need, and so bit by bit he gave all his precious gift away to these needy people, and he never did make it to Bethlehem. But did he deliver his offering or not? And did it matter that he didn't reach his intended destination?

These are questions we might ask ourselves as we reflect on whether faith is about being saved or being spent.

. . . Am I Really Free?

We may live in what we like to call a free country and enjoy freedom of speech and movement, which our fore-bears fought bitter wars to gain and maintain. But are we really free?

Many people would say that freedom means being able to do what you like as long as you don't harm others, or being able to organize your life as you wish without having to be accountable to anyone else.

A person of faith sees freedom differently. Spiritual free-dom is the ability to live in balance with all created things so that you can enjoy and use them responsibly without becoming dependent on them. It's about holding lightly to what you think you own so that if the need arises, you can let it go. It's about traveling light along the pioneer pathways of life, so that your baggage doesn't make it impossible for you to move on.

Two employees worked for the same boss, whose methods were sometimes dishonest and unscrupulous. One day one of them refused to carry out the boss's instructions, and he was fired. The other obeyed orders and was promoted. Afterward, the second employee said to the first: "You fool. If you could only learn to obey his orders, you wouldn't have to live so frugally now." And the second replied, "And if you could only learn to live frugally, you wouldn't have to obey his orders."

Which one of them was free?

Are there any invisible chains around your life that are holding you captive in situations, or compulsions that prevent you from growing and becoming the person God is dreaming you to be?

And You?

How do you feel about these questions?

Are there any questions you feel you need to ask yourself?

Can you let them arise in your prayer conversations with God?

Learn from yesterday, live for today, hope for tomorrow. The important thing is not to stop questioning.
—Albert Einstein

15
I Believe . . .

. . . That what I see is not all there is and that underpinning all that I call reality is a mystery infinitely greater and wiser than I am.

. . . That this mystery causes all things to unfold in wisdom and toward the greater fullness of life, that this mystery means well with us and strives constantly to bring the more life-giving outcome from all that happens, drawing our poor to better and our better to best. I call this mystery God. Yet I see the effects of the opposite dynamic also at work, dragging our best down to mediocre and our poor to worst. Everything in the story so far convinces me that life will prevail over death and light over darkness.

. . . That we are all invited to cooperate in this great adventure we call life, as partners in the ongoing creativity of God on planet Earth, and that we have the power within us to choose, continually, the drawing of God over the drag of the darkness. I believe this is what *discernment* means.

. . . That two thousand years ago a child called Jesus was born to humble parents in the Middle East, that in his life he revealed what the fullness of God's unfolding dream looks like in human form when it is fully evolved, showing us the way to live so that our lives, too, reveal and incarnate some small but uniquely precious fragment of God's dream for humanity.

. . . That Jesus was killed on the cross because he lived absolutely true to God's dream for life on the earth and thus challenged the powers of darkness and the systems of domination of his time, and that those same powers of darkness and domination destroyed his earthly life. I believe that this is the cost of living true to God's dream, that the dynamic of darkness lurks both within us and beyond us, and that anyone who tries to live true to God in his or her own life will also encounter a cross in some form.

. . . That although Jesus died, he transcended death in ways we cannot understand, and that his Spirit lives on and flows through the lives of all who are willing to be channels for that transforming power.

. . . That it doesn't matter so much what I believe *about* Jesus, as it does that I am willing to *follow* in the path he models, knowing what it may cost. I believe that if I do try to follow him, his Spirit will constantly guide, energize, and shape my journey and that of the whole human family.

. . . That, although I am an individual, called to give expression to some fragment of God's dream, I have no meaning except in relationship. I believe that the relationship among God the source of all being, Jesus the one who reveals this mystery in human form, and the Spirit who brings the source of life into our everyday living is a model of a relationship in which all of us are called to participate, a dance of life we are invited to join.

. . . That, at the end of the day, "to believe" means to trust the mystery I call God and not try to define it.

Try writing your own "I believe . . ."

Also Available

From satisfying work to sudden unemployment. From a happy marriage to a hurtful divorce. From caring for the kids to caring for an aging parent. These are just a few of the countless ways that life hurls us into the chaos of change, where our certainties are shaken and our faith may even begin to falter. But what if we saw the chaos—the "mess"—of our lives not as something to fear or eschew, but as something to be embraced?

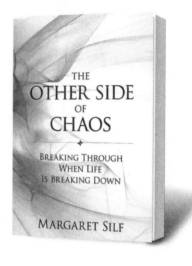

Margaret Silf
$13.95 • pb • 3308-1

In *The Other Side of Chaos,* bestselling author Margaret Silf looks closely at the subject of chaos—and the intrinsic transition it brings—through the lens of Christian spirituality. Through Scripture stories and verses, personal accounts, and other anecdotes, Silf helps us develop an authentic "spirituality of transition" that leads us to live out life's changes constructively, creatively, and confidently.

To order, call 800-621-1008,
visit www.loyolapress.com/store,
or go to your local bookseller.

LOYOLAPRESS.
A JESUIT MINISTRY

Also Available

Anyone seeking to deepen his or her relationship with God will greatly benefit from *Inner Compass*, Margaret Silf's dynamic presentation of the profound insights of St. Ignatius of Loyola's Spiritual Exercises. While reflective, the work exudes a congenial, practical outlook and a thoroughly modern sensibility. As Silf points out, the book "grew out of questions rather than certainty, discovery rather than doctrine, the experience of everyday living rather than academic study."

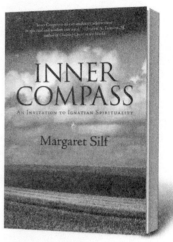

Margaret Silf
$14.95 • pb • 2645-8

This 10th-anniversary edition of the acclaimed *Inner Compass* features a new introduction and personal invitation to the reader, plus a significantly expanded resource section. Devoted followers of Ignatian spirituality and spiritual seekers alike will find that wherever life has led them, *Inner Compass* offers renewed direction and purpose and helps them recognize the will of God within their own hearts.

To order, call 800-621-1008,
visit www.loyolapress.com/store,
or go to your local bookseller.

LOYOLAPRESS.
A JESUIT MINISTRY

Also Available

In *Compass Points*, best-selling Ignatian spirituality author Margaret Silf enables us to see God beyond the grandiose and introduces us to the Divine in our daily lives. Through short but powerful meditations rooted in Ignatian spirituality and through vignettes based on her own authentic spiritual experiences, Silf reveals the interior process of Ignatian mindfulness—a core tenet of which is that God can be found in all things. By joining Silf on her journey through real life in the real world, our eyes, minds, and hearts are opened to the Divine experience, and we come to recognize God's active presence in everything that we do.

Margaret Silf
$13.95 • pb • 2810-0